Sovereign Field Series

Clarity

A J Moore | Sovereign Frequency

Published by Action Consulting & Media Group

ISBN: 978-1-972967-06-5

Introduction

Clarity is not something you achieve. It is something you return to when distortion loosens its grip.

Clarity does not require force. It requires recognition.

Complete each section in order. This is a full clarity pass.

Section I — Work / Professional

Pause. Now breathe. Nothing here requires collapse.

Clarity Pass 1

What event occurred?

____

____

____

What emotion arose?

____

____

____

What did I assume?

____

____

____

What did I predict?

____

____

____

What feels urgent?

____

____

What evidence supports this?

____

____

What evidence does not?

____

____

What can remain undecided?

____

____

What requires action today?

____

____

What is optional?

____

____

____

Work friction is measurable and predictable. Choose alignment over force.

Section II — Personal Life

Release urgency. This is communication. The goal is to
understand, not win.

Clarity Pass 1

What event occurred?

What emotion arose?

What did I assume?

What did I predict?

What feels urgent?

____

____

What evidence supports this?

____

____

What evidence does not?

____

____

What can remain undecided?

____

____

What requires action today?

____

____

What is optional?

____

____

____

I choose what aligns with my truth and peace.

Section III — Relationships

Pause. Incomplete information cannot support a clear decision.

Clarity Pass 1

What event occurred?

What emotion arose?

What did I assume?

What did I predict?

What feels urgent?

What evidence supports this?

What evidence does not?

What can remain undecided?

What requires action today?

What is optional?

____

____

____

Truth is information. I use it to make aligned decisions.

Section IV — Financial

Breathe. Pressure is not authority.

Clarity Pass 1

What event occurred?

What emotion arose?

What did I assume?

What did I predict?

What feels urgent?

What evidence supports this?

What evidence does not?

What can remain undecided?

What requires action today?

What is optional?

____

____

____

Nothing defines me without my permission. I decide what this means.

Section V — Internal / Self

Am I safe right now? Pause. Breathe.

Clarity Pass 1

What is objectively true?

____

____

____

What is assumed?

____

____

____

What is emotionally amplified?

____

____

____

What is within my control?

____

____

____

What requires action today?

____

____

____

What can be released?

____

____

____

What is the clearest next step?

____

____

____

I am safe. I am clear. I execute from here.

— Begin Clarity Pass 2 —

Section I — Work / Professional
Pause. Now breathe. Nothing here requires collapse.

Clarity Pass 2
What event occurred?

What emotion arose?

What did I assume?

What did I predict?

What feels urgent?

What evidence supports this?

What evidence does not?

What can remain undecided?

What requires action today?

What is optional?

____

____

____

Work friction is measurable and predictable. Choose alignment over force.

Section II — Personal Life

Release urgency. This is communication. The goal is to understand, not win.

Clarity Pass 2

What event occurred?

____

____

____

What emotion arose?

____

____

____

What did I assume?

____

____

____

What did I predict?

____

____

____

What feels urgent?

____

____

____

What evidence supports this?

____

____

____

What evidence does not?

____

____

____

What can remain undecided?

____

____

____

What requires action today?

____

____

____

What is optional?

____

____

____

I choose what aligns with my truth and peace.

Section III — Relationships

Pause. Incomplete information cannot support a clear decision.

Clarity Pass 2

What event occurred?

What emotion arose?

What did I assume?

What did I predict?

What feels urgent?

What evidence supports this?

What evidence does not?

What can remain undecided?

What requires action today?

What is optional?

____

____

____

Truth is information. I use it to make aligned decisions.

Section IV — Financial

Breathe. Pressure is not authority.

Clarity Pass 2

What event occurred?

What emotion arose?

What did I assume?

What did I predict?

What feels urgent?

____

____

What evidence supports this?

____

____

What evidence does not?

____

____

What can remain undecided?

____

____

What requires action today?

____

____

What is optional?

____

____

____

Nothing defines me without my permission. I decide what this means.

Section V — Internal / Self

Am I safe right now? Pause. Breathe.

Clarity Pass 2

What is objectively true?

What is assumed?

What is emotionally amplified?

What is within my control?

What requires action today?

____

____

____

What can be released?

____

____

____

What is the clearest next step?

____

____

____

I am safe. I am clear. I execute from here.

— Begin Clarity Pass 3 —

Section I — Work / Professional

Pause. Now breathe. Nothing here requires collapse.

Clarity Pass 3

What event occurred?

____

____

____

What emotion arose?

____

____

____

What did I assume?

____

____

____

What did I predict?

____

____

____

What feels urgent?

____

____

____

What evidence supports this?

____

____

____

What evidence does not?

____

____

____

What can remain undecided?

____

____

____

What requires action today?

____

____

____

What is optional?

____

____

____

Work friction is measurable and predictable. Choose alignment over force.

Section II — Personal Life

Release urgency. This is communication. The goal is to understand, not win.

Clarity Pass 3

What event occurred?

______

What emotion arose?

______

What did I assume?

______

What did I predict?

______

What feels urgent?

____

____

What evidence supports this?

____

____

What evidence does not?

____

____

What can remain undecided?

____

____

What requires action today?

____

____

What is optional?

____

____

____

I choose what aligns with my truth and peace.

Section III — Relationships

Pause. Incomplete information cannot support a clear decision.

Clarity Pass 3

What event occurred?

____

____

____

What emotion arose?

____

____

____

What did I assume?

____

____

____

What did I predict?

____

____

____

What feels urgent?

____

____

____

What evidence supports this?

____

____

____

What evidence does not?

____

____

____

What can remain undecided?

____

____

____

What requires action today?

____

____

____

What is optional?

____

____

____

Truth is information. I use it to make aligned decisions.

Section IV — Financial

Breathe. Pressure is not authority.

Clarity Pass 3

What event occurred?

What emotion arose?

What did I assume?

What did I predict?

What feels urgent?

____

____

____

What evidence supports this?

____

____

____

What evidence does not?

____

____

____

What can remain undecided?

____

____

____

What requires action today?

____

____

____

What is optional?

____

____

____

Nothing defines me without my permission. I decide what this means.

Section V — Internal / Self

Am I safe right now? Pause. Breathe.

Clarity Pass 3

What is objectively true?

____

____

____

What is assumed?

____

____

____

What is emotionally amplified?

____

____

____

What is within my control?

____

____

____

What requires action today?

What can be released?

What is the clearest next step?

I am safe. I am clear. I execute from here.

Closing Note

You do not need to control everything to be sovereign.

You need to see clearly enough to choose.

Return as often as needed.